iScience
Science in the Real World

Weather and the Water Cycle

by Emily Sohn and Erin Ash Sullivan

NorwoodHousePress
Chicago, Illinois

Norwood House Press
Chicago, Illinois

For information regarding Norwood House Press, please visit our website at
www.norwoodhousepress.com or call 866-565-2900.

Contributor: Edward Rock, Project Content Consultant
Editor: Lauren Dupuis-Perez
Designer: Sara Radka
Fact Checker: Sam Rhodes

Photo Credits in this revised edition include: Getty Images: DigitalVision, 25, DigitalVision,
35, iStockphoto, cover, 1, 38, Koichi Kamoshida, 23, Moment, 5, 14: Pixabay: Byunilho,
background (paper texture), GDJ, background (tech pattern); Shutterstock: Dmitry
Naumov, 17, Fineart1, 22, FrameStockFootages, 34, Gorodisskij, 32 (bottom); Wikimedia:
Fenners, 16

Library of Congress Cataloging-in-Publication Data

Names: Sohn, Emily, author. | Sullivan, Erin Ash, author. | Sohn, Emily. iScience.
Title: Weather and the water cycle / by Emily Sohn and Erin Ash Sullivan.
Description: [2019 edition]. | Chicago, Illinois : Norwood House Press, [2019] | Series: iScience
    | Audience: Grades 4 to 6. | Includes bibliographical references and index.
Identifiers: LCCN 2018058149 | ISBN 9781684509430 (hardcover) |
    ISBN 9781684044092 (pbk.) | ISBN 9781684044207 (ebook)
Subjects: LCSH: Weather forecasting—Juvenile literature.
    | Hydrologic cycle—Juvenile literature.
Classification: LCC QC995.43 .S64 2019 | DDC 551.57—dc23
LC record available at https://lccn.loc.gov/2018058149

Hardcover ISBN: 978-1-68450-943-0
Paperback ISBN: 978-1-68404-409-2

Contents

Note to Caregivers:

In this updated and revised iScience series, each book poses many questions to the reader. Some are open ended and ask what the reader thinks. Discuss these questions with your child and guide him or her in thinking through the possible answers and outcomes. There are also questions posed which have a specific answer. Encourage your child to read through the text to determine the correct answer. Most importantly, throughout the book, encourage answers using critical thinking skills and imagination. In the back of the book you will find answers to these questions, along with additional resources to help support you as you share the book with your child.

Words that are **bolded** are defined in the glossary in the back of the book.

What Is the Weather?

Before you get dressed, it helps to check the weather. Will it be cold or hot? Cloudy or sunny? People want to **predict** the weather for other reasons, too. Farmers need to know when to plant their crops. Athletes look to see if their games will be rained out. How does the weather affect your daily life? In this book, you will learn the best ways to predict weather and make your own **forecast**!

Predicting the Weather

Your class is planning a school fair. The day will be full of games and races outside at a nearby park. On the afternoon before the fair, the sky is full of clouds. Will rain ruin the fair? How can you be sure?

Solution 1: Look at the Clouds

Some clouds carry rain, while others do not. Knowing which clouds are which can help you predict the weather.

Solution 2: Use a Barometer

A **barometer** is a tool for measuring **air pressure**. Information about air pressure can help you predict the weather.

Solution 3: Use a Thermometer

A thermometer is a tool that measures temperature. Knowing how hot or cold it is can tell you what to expect.

Solution 4: Use a Weather Map

Some weather maps show pictures of Earth as seen from far away. They show what is happening in the sky.

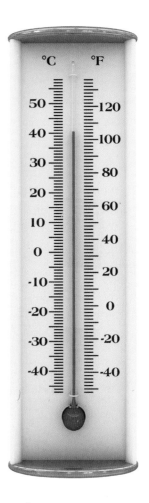

Before you try to solve the puzzle, ask yourself these questions:
· When is it important to predict the weather?
· Why is it important to watch the evening weather report on television or check it on the internet?
· What conditions tell you the most about what kind of weather is coming?
· Why do you think it is important to understand how weather works?

Discover Activity

Make It Rain

Materials
- a large plastic bowl
- a small plastic cup or bowl (shorter than the large bowl)
- plastic wrap
- warm water
- a small rock
- a large paper clip

To become a weather expert, you need to know about water. That's because water covers 71 percent of Earth's surface. As water moves between land and sky, weather patterns change positions, or shift.

large plastic bowl

small plastic bowl

Water can be a solid, a liquid, or a gas. It changes form in a process called the **water cycle**. To get into the groove of the water cycle, try the following activity.

plastic wrap

paper clip

small rock

Make a model to see how the water cycle works. Put 0.25 inches (0.635 centimeters) of warm water in the bowl. Put a small cup in the middle of the bowl. The cup should be right side up. Use a rock inside the cup to hold it down. Cover the bowl tightly with plastic wrap. Place a paper clip on the plastic above the cup so the plastic dips a bit. Now, put the bowl indoors in strong sunlight. Check on the model every 15 minutes for a few hours. Write down what you observe. Now try the same thing, but keep the bowl in the dark. How do the results differ?

Imagine that the bowl is a lake. What happens to the lake water on a sunny day? What does the model teach you about weather?

What Causes Rain?

Before rain can fall, water has to get up into the sky. To do this, water gets help from the Sun. The Sun's energy causes water to evaporate. **Water vapor** describes tiny particles of water that float in the air. These droplets are all around you. They are too small to see. But they can move.

These clouds are heavy with condensed water drops. By their color, you can tell it will rain soon.

First, water vapor uses warm air to go up. Warm air is good at holding lots of water. It is also lighter than cool air, so it rises. When warm, water-filled air gets high enough, it cools down. Cold air cannot hold as much water vapor as warm air can. As a result, some of the vapor condenses, or turns back into a liquid. This liquid clings to specks of dust in the air, forming tiny droplets of water.

Without windshield wipers, drivers would have a hard time seeing in the rain. Can you see through this windshield?

Clouds form when many tiny droplets of water group together. Within a cloud, some droplets bump into each other. They merge into larger droplets. Sometimes the clouds become so full of water droplets that the air cannot hold them up. Then they fall to the ground as raindrops or snow, depending on the temperature. Rain and snow are different types of **precipitation**.

Think about Solution 1 of the iScience Puzzle. How might looking at clouds help you predict the weather?

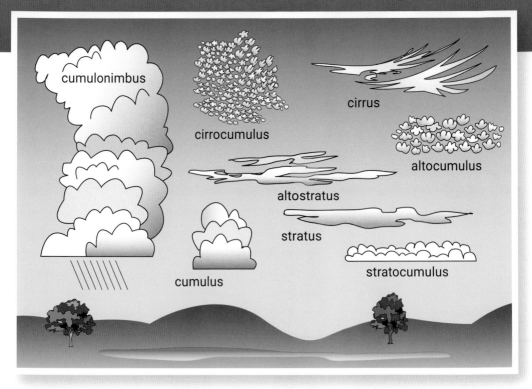

Over the next few days, see if you can find some of these clouds in the sky where you live.

What Are Some Types of Clouds?

You could look at the sky every day for a year and never see two clouds that look exactly the same. Some clouds are more likely to bring rain than others. Knowing which clouds are stormiest can help you predict the weather.

One helpful clue is to see how high in the sky clouds are. Cirrus clouds are the farthest from Earth's surface. They form above 18,000 feet (5,486 meters). Altostratus clouds are a little lower, lying between 6,500 feet (1,981 m) and 18,000 feet. Stratus clouds are the lowest, floating below 6,500 feet.

Through the window of an airplane, it often looks like a beautiful, sunny day. That's true even if it is cloudy and rainy down below. Why might this be?

When you see nimbostratus clouds like this coming your way, take cover or prepare to get wet!

Clouds can tell you a lot about the weather if you look closely at them. Clouds that are thin, wispy, and float high in the sky are called cumulus clouds. On sunny days, they look like puffs of cotton. Cumulus clouds appear only during good weather.

On the other hand, dark gray clouds are signs that trouble is brewing. These clouds cover the sky in sheets. They are called altostratus. Nimbostratus clouds look the same but are a little lower in the sky.

Think about how water droplets form and combine in clouds. Which kinds of clouds would be more likely to rain on your school fair?

Where Does Wind Come From?

Whoosh! Like clouds, wind can also help you predict weather. Wind often blows clouds through the sky. That can lead to a change in the weather.

The breeze blows over the ocean to replace the warm air rising over the land.

Breezes are common near the ocean. Here's why: During a day at the beach, energy from the Sun warms the land more quickly than it warms the water. Warm, dry air rises over the land. To replace this rising air, breezes blow from the ocean toward the land.

What do you think ocean breezes feel like?

Would the pages of this book blow from left to right or right to left in the evening? Hint: Look at where the ocean is.

At night, everything happens in reverse. As the Sun goes down, the land cools much more quickly than the seawater does. Now, warm air rises over the ocean. To replace it, cool air blows from the land back out over the ocean.

Because breezes are so common near the ocean, temperatures remain fairly steady there. Coastal areas have fewer extremely hot and cold days than **inland** areas do. The Great Lakes in the Midwest create their own patterns. As storms come in from the west and pass over the lakes, they pick up water. This water falls out as rain or snow just east of the lakes.

Where does it rain or snow more: along ocean shores or inland?

Thermometers

A thermometer measures how hot or cold something is. Thermometers use materials that change in some way when they are heated or cooled. We use thermometers to determine how warm or cold the air is, to check body temperature, and even to determine if food is cooked all the way.

Before modern thermometers were invented, there was a device called a thermoscope. It could show that something was getting hotter or colder, but it could not determine its exact temperature. Scientists Santorio and Galileo were the first to put numbers on a thermoscope, but they were not accurate temperature gauges.

a Galileo thermoscope

The thermometer we still use today was invented by Daniel Gabriel Fahrenheit. Fahrenheit made a thermometer that contained alcohol and one that contained mercury. Fahrenheit's most significant contribution on measuring temperature was the creation of an accurate numeric scale in 1724. He chose 32 degrees as the temperature for freezing water. The boiling point of water was set at 212 degrees.

In 1742, astronomer Anders Celsius introduced the centigrade scale. It is also known as the Celsius scale. The Celsius scale has 0 degrees as the freezing point of water, and 100 degrees as the boiling point.

Fahrenheit's scale is still used today in the United States. The Celsius scale is used throughout the rest of the world.

Mountain Weather

You've stared at the clouds and felt the wind. Now look at the land around you. **Landforms** play a role in weather prediction. Is it very flat where you live? Or are there mountains nearby? The answer will tell you something about the weather.

These mountains block the movement of clouds.

Mountains are so tall that they block some clouds from moving past them. As a result, special weather patterns develop in mountainous areas. First, warm, moist air moves up a mountain slope. As the warm air rises, it cools. Remember that cool air can't hold as much water vapor as warm air can. When water vapor condenses, clouds form and rain or snow falls.

Which side of the mountains in the distance is this farm probably on—the west side or the east side? Why?

Wind and weather systems often move from west to east in North America. As clouds move, the western slopes and tops of mountains get the most rain and snow.

As air moves down the east side of the mountain, it gets warmer. But the air stays very dry because all of the water vapor has already fallen out of it. Very little rain falls on an eastern mountain slope. This area is known as a **rain shadow**. It is **arid** there.

Hundreds of years ago, early settlers moved west across America. Along their journeys, these people had to decide where to build their homes and farms. How could knowing about mountain weather have helped them?

Umatilla Rock is in the rain shadow region east of the Cascade Mountains in Washington state. Look for it and the Cascades on a map of Washington state. Can you figure out where the rain shadow is?

How Are Deserts Formed?

Wet weather is unlikely to cancel your school fair if you live in a desert. A desert is an area that receives very little rain. Some deserts lie in the rain shadow of mountains. In Washington state, for example, a desert region lies just east of the Cascade Mountains. Death Valley is one of the driest places on Earth. It lies east of two mountain ranges in California.

Deserts often form near the centers of continents. They can be really hot. That's because air gets warmer and drier as it moves across land. Deserts make up much of inland Australia.

What kinds of activities might be difficult for people to do in desert regions?

Deserts also tend to lie just north and south of the equator. That's the band around the center of Earth that gets the most direct sunlight. Because of the way wind patterns blow around Earth, warm, wet air gathers around the equator. As water vapor condenses from the air, heavy rains drench rain forests in Ecuador, Brazil, and other places. Once it has dumped all the water out, warm air blows north and south into nearby deserts.

Do you live near any desert environments? If so, why do you think they formed there? If you were planning a school fair in the desert, what kinds of weather worries might you have?

This desert region is a harsh environment. But some plants and animals still manage to live here.

Climatologist

Weather is ever-changing and often temporary. A rainstorm can last a few minutes or a few days. A tornado comes and goes quickly. Even seasons give way to hotter or colder temperatures. But climate is the combined weather conditions of an area over a long period of time. Climate is all the weather in a place, season after season, combined.

Climatologists collect information at weather stations.

A meteorologist predicts the weather, but a climatologist studies the trends and patterns of weather over time. Climatologists might study weather patterns that happen over a period of years, or even centuries. They gather data from weather stations and satellites. They also study factors that affect weather, and the ways weather affects the environment.

Climatologists are experts on climate change. They study ancient rocks and ice cores to understand how weather patterns have changed over time. They try to understand future weather patterns. Climatologists investigate ocean temperatures, depths, and currents. They even study volcanoes. They use their observations to make predictions.

Everything from agriculture to our health is affected by the climate. Climatologists help us understand how weather patterns affect life in a particular area.

a 1-million-year-old ice core

How Does the Water Cycle Affect Weather?

On rainy days, puddles form. When the Sun comes out, the puddles disappear. This is just one example of the never-ending movement of water on our planet. It is called the water cycle. As long as the Sun continues to emit heat, water will keep changing form, or **state**. In turn, weather will keep changing.

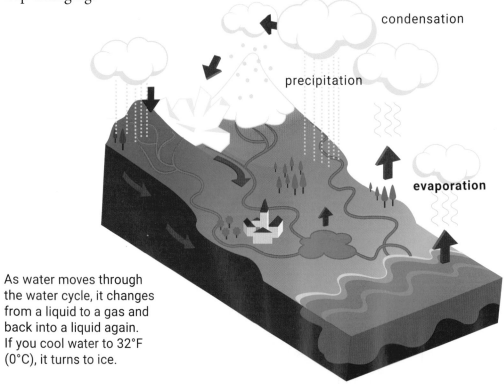

condensation

precipitation

evaporation

As water moves through the water cycle, it changes from a liquid to a gas and back into a liquid again. If you cool water to 32°F (0°C), it turns to ice.

Puddles disappear when the Sun shines on the water. Molecules of water absorb the Sun's energy. They get warmer and move faster. Eventually, the liquid turns to water vapor. This process is called evaporation.

Eventually, most of the water in this puddle will change to water vapor and rise into the atmosphere.

Huge amounts of water are constantly evaporating from oceans, lakes, and rivers. Wind speeds up the process. As water turns to vapor, it enters the atmosphere. It builds up. And it moves with wind and clouds. After a while, water vapor condenses. It falls as rain or snow. The water cycle continues.

Remember the bowl of water in the Discover Activity? What did you learn about evaporation in that investigation?

Under the right conditions, this ice will seem to disappear without melting first. It will change directly into a gas.

Did You Know?

Plants also participate in the water cycle. Water moves through roots and stems to the plants' leaves. Some of this water evaporates. **Transpiration** is the process of water escaping from leaves in the form of water vapor.

Winter does wondrous things to water. When it's cold enough, liquid water will become a solid when it turns to ice or snow. These crystals and flakes have tricks up their sleeves, too. Ice and snow can vanish without a trace! **Sublimation** is when solid water becomes water vapor without going through the liquid state first. Sometimes snow slowly disappears under dry conditions, even when it is too cold to melt. It's not magic. It's sublimation.

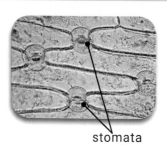

Plants lose water through transpiration. Water exits a plant through tiny holes, called stomata, in its leaves.

stomata

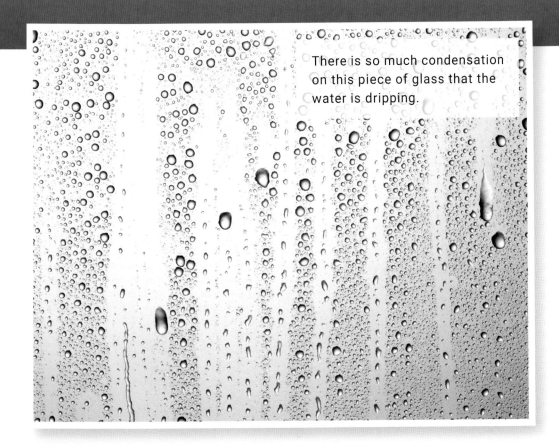

There is so much condensation on this piece of glass that the water is dripping.

What Goes Up Must Come Down

Evaporation and **condensation** are like two kids on a seesaw. Together, they keep the water cycle going. Both depend on energy from the Sun to work. Remember that evaporation puts water vapor into the air. Warm air rises, like a kid going up on the seesaw. Once up there, the air cools down. Now, it can't hold as much water vapor. So, the vapor condenses, or turns back into a liquid. Water drops form around dust particles and become clouds. Now, the seesaw goes the other way. Precipitation comes down.

Think back to the Discover Activity. Where did condensation occur in the model? Which part of the model represents clouds?

What Is Precipitation?

No matter where you live, you've probably seen some kind of moisture fall out of the sky. This is precipitation, the stage that follows condensation in the water cycle.

When it's warm out, precipitation falls as rain. When the air temperature drops, rain turns to sleet or hail. At very cold temperatures, ice crystals form and become snowflakes. To predict what type of precipitation might fall on the day of the school fair, you will need to know the air temperature.

Think about Solution 3 to the iScience Puzzle. Can a thermometer help you predict the weather for your school fair? Will the temperature alone tell you if precipitation is going to fall?

Most precipitation that falls is in the form of rain. But the right conditions can produce sleet, hail, or snow.

Polar bears normally walk long distances on the ice, hunting for seals. As the ice melts, their hunting territory gets smaller and smaller.

Moving Water

On Earth, the oceans store a whole lot of water. And most precipitation falls right back over the oceans.

Water storage also happens in ice caps near the North and South poles. Some ice has been frozen there for thousands of years. Scientists pay close attention to the amount of ice at the poles. In recent years, ice caps have been melting.

What could melting ice caps do to the oceans? How might a rise or fall in sea level affect coastal areas? What about inland areas?

When snow melts in the mountains, the water runs downhill and meets up with other streams and rivers.

Snow can pile up for months in cold places. But when spring finally arrives, snow turns to water. Often, that water gets moving. At the tops of mountains, **snowmelt** runs downhill. It flows into lakes, streams, and rivers.

In warm places, rain behaves much like snowmelt. **Runoff** makes its way downhill. Small bodies of water meet up with larger bodies of water. Over time, water evaporates from streams, rivers, and standing pools. Again, the water cycle continues.

Some water soaks into the ground after it falls to Earth. Runoff and snowmelt can seep into soil and cracks in rocks, much like dishwater into a sponge. This is called **infiltration**. Water that has infiltrated the ground is called **groundwater**.

Aquifers are areas of rock, dirt, or sand that naturally store water underground. We get much of our freshwater supply from aquifers, so they are very important to us. But there are dangers.

Toxic materials such as paint and chemicals can leak out of **landfills**. When that happens, they pollute aquifers and poison groundwater. That is one reason to be concerned about what goes into landfills.

Do you know where your water comes from?

This man is checking the level of groundwater in an area.

Water evaporates faster when it is hot, like in this natural spring.

Sometimes, groundwater **saturates** the ground so much that water breaks through to the surface. This is where you find natural springs.

Think about the model of the water cycle you made in the Discover Activity. How could you change it to make aquifers and springs? It's sublimation.

People can relax in hot springs that are not too hot.

Jet streams are winds that travel high in Earth's atmosphere.

How Do We Predict Weather?

Meteorologists are scientists who study the weather. By observing winds, temperature, and precipitation patterns, they can attempt to predict the weather after analyzing data.

Meteorologists pay close attention to jet streams—strong, fast winds that wrap around Earth. These winds whip around at up to 200 miles (322 kilometers) per hour!

Jet streams form as cold winds from the North and South poles run into warmer winds from closer to the equator. The difference in temperature is what causes the strong winds. As the temperature difference gets bigger, the winds grow stronger. How would a jet stream affect the speed of a flying airplane?

These meteorologists are tracking a storm.

Jet streams are strong enough to move clouds and weather systems. Meteorologists watch weather move along the jet streams. That helps them predict what is coming your way.

Jet streams travel from west to east. They rush along very high above the surface of Earth. With that in mind, which way would most weather travel?

A Moving Force

A storm is like a marching band. The leading edge is called a **front**. Looking for storm fronts can help you predict weather a few days ahead of time.

A warm front describes a mass of warm air approaching a mass of cooler air. When the two masses meet, the lighter warm air moves over the heavier cool air. A warm front can bring fog, rain, or snow.

A cold front describes a mass of cool air approaching a warmer air mass. The heavier cool air slides under the warm air and forces it to rise. A cold front can bring cloudy weather, big rainstorms, heavy snowstorms, and more. The amount of precipitation that falls depends on the amount of water vapor in the warm air.

Fronts can sometimes mean lots of snow to play in.

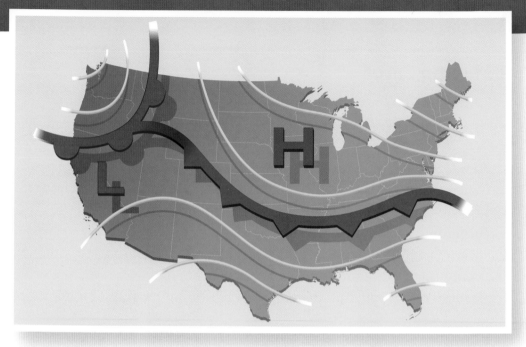

A warm front is shown on a weather map as a line with red half circles that point in the direction the front is traveling. A cold front is a line with blue triangles pointed in the direction the front is moving. What would happen on a warm spring day where the two fronts meet on the map?

Sometimes, a meeting of air masses results in a standstill. Neither mass has the energy to move around the other. This is called a stationary front. It just sits there, leading to many days of cloudy, rainy, or snowy weather.

Other times, air masses act like sandwiches. Two cool air masses can squish a warm air mass between them. Then the cool air moves under the warmer air from both sides. The warm air gets cut off from the ground. This is called an occluded front. It causes temperatures to drop. Rain or snow may fall.

Imagine that the school fair is happening on a hot day. A warm front that is heavy with water vapor is approaching. What kind of weather is likely?

Under Pressure

Whether it's hot or cold, wet or dry, weather reports often mention air pressure. This describes the weight of air pushing down on Earth. Barometers measure air pressure. Air pressure tells a lot about what kind of weather is coming.

When air pressure rises, air tends to sink. As it gets closer to the ground, the air gets warmer. Now, it can hold more water vapor. As a result, clouds do not form and there are no storms. An H on a weather map points to high pressure air masses. You can expect calm weather there.

With the air pressure as it is shown on this barometer, what is the weather likely to be?

High barometric pressure brings calm days and fun times!

When air pressure drops, air tends to rise. On its way up, it gets colder. Water vapor in the air condenses into clouds. That leads to precipitation. An L marks low-pressure systems on the weather map. Storms are often connected to these conditions. Barometric pressure is very low inside a hurricane.

Think about what high-pressure days are like through the seasons in the area where you live. What activities might you plan for winter days when high pressure is in the forecast? What might you plan for high-pressure days in the summer? Now think about what low-pressure days are like. What activities might you like to do when low pressure is in the forecast?

Would it be better for the air pressure to be high or low on the day of your school fair? Remember, the school fair is scheduled to take place outdoors.

On low-pressure days, it's time for some indoor fun.

= warm front
= cold front

What do you think would be happening in the upper left corner in winter?

When a high-pressure system meets a low-pressure system, winds pick up. The wind blows along the boundary between the two systems. You might feel strong winds when a front moves through.

Think about Solution 4 of the iScience Puzzle. How can the map help you predict the weather?

Tools of the Trade

You can make some good guesses about the weather just by looking at clouds and landscapes and feeling the wind. But meteorologists get extra help from detailed maps.

Some of these maps show pictures taken by **weather satellites** in space. Some satellites are **geostationary**. They orbit Earth at the same rate as Earth rotates. So they are always above the same place. Other satellites orbit from the North Pole to the South Pole and back again. Together, they show the weather in just about every spot on Earth.

How could a satellite map help you decide whether it will rain on the day of the school fair?

A satellite like the one in this computer-simulated image takes pictures of Earth's surface. Meteorologists can tell by the pictures what weather patterns are occurring.

This tower sends out radio waves and records how long they take to bounce back from a distant weather object.

Meteorologists also use **radar**. An antenna sends radio waves toward rain clouds or another weather object. (A weather object could be a mass of clouds, a rainstorm, a snowstorm, a hurricane, or the like.) A tool records how long it takes for the waves to bounce back. Meteorologists know how fast radio waves move. So they can tell how far away the rain clouds are and how fast they are moving. That information tells meteorologists where the weather object is. Repeated readings keep track of the rain clouds over time.

Today, weather experts use a new system. It's called Doppler radar. It can detect the movement of material in the air. That shows where weather systems are heading, and how quickly.

How could Doppler radar help you decide if it is going to rain for the school fair?

Solve the ⓘScience Puzzle

Here is what some experts have to say about each possible solution. Where do your ideas agree or disagree?

Solution 1: Look at the Clouds

Pros: Clouds offer good clues about the weather over the next 12 to 24 hours.

Cons: The wind might speed up or slow down. So, new weather could blow in.

Solution 2: Use a Barometer

Pros: Knowing if air pressure is high or low can tell you if you can expect weather to be calm or stormy. If the pressure is dropping or rising, you can also tell if storms are building or clearing up.

Cons: A barometer will not show if the air is humid or dry. And it can't tell you whether it's hot or cold out.

Solution 3: Use a Thermometer

Pros: Knowing the temperature will help you look for patterns in the week's weather.

Cons: Today's temperature will not tell you if rain or sunshine is on the way.

Solution 4: Use a Weather Map

Pros: A weather map provides a great deal of information.

Cons: Weather maps can be hard to read if you don't have practice.

Can you use a combination of solutions to predict the weather? Which methods would work best where you live?

Beyond the Puzzle

You have learned how water moves from land to sky and back again. You have seen how this cycle affects weather patterns. Now, it's your turn to be a meteorologist. Look in your local newspaper or on the internet for weather maps of your area. Make sure the maps show fronts and temperatures. Using just the pictures, try to predict the weather for the next few days. Now check your answers against the real forecast. Over the next few days, see whose forecast is right. Try this for a week or two. Did you get any better at predicting the weather?

Now that you are a weather expert, you can amaze your family and friends with your own forecasts and predictions!

What kinds of weather tools will you use when you make your predictions? Maps? Satellite images? Anything else?

Glossary

air pressure: the force air exerts on a specific area.

aquifers: areas deep under the ground where water is naturally stored.

arid: very dry.

barometer: a tool for measuring air pressure.

condensation: the stage in water cycle when water vapor turns to liquid.

evaporation: the stage in water cycle when liquid water turns to vapor.

forecast: a prediction of what the weather will be in the days ahead.

front: the leading edge of a weather system.

geostationary: orbiting Earth at the same rate as Earth rotates, which gives a satellite the appearance of standing still.

groundwater: water in the water cycle that is stored under the ground.

infiltration: when water soaks deep into Earth and is stored underground.

inland: away from the ocean.

jet streams: thin bands of strong winds high in Earth's atmosphere.

landfills: areas of land in which garbage and trash are buried.

landforms: features of Earth, such as mountains or deserts.

meteorologists: scientists who study weather.

precipitation: the stage in water cycle when water falls from clouds.

predict: to tell what might happen in the future.

radar: a tool for measuring distance using radio waves.

rain shadow: the side of a mountain that receives very little rain.

runoff: rainwater that makes its way downhill to a body of water.

saturates: soaks all the way through.

snowmelt: melted snow that goes back into the water cycle.

springs: places where water from aquifers comes to the surface.

state: the form that a substance takes, such as solid, liquid, or gas.

sublimation: a process in which ice and snow turn into water vapor without melting first.

transpiration: a plant process in which water goes through roots, stems, and leaves, and into the air.

water cycle: the process of water changing its form and moving around Earth.

water vapor: water in the gaseous state.

weather satellites: spacecraft that orbit Earth and gather information about weather conditions.

Further Reading

Hayes, Amy. 2019. *Earth's Hydrosphere.* Understanding Earth's Systems. New York: PowerKids Press.

Kenney, Karen Latchana. 2019. *Meteorologist.* STEM Careers. Minneapolis, Minn.: Jump!, Inc.

NASA Climate Kids. **Weather and Climate.** https://climatekids.nasa.gov/menu/weather-and-climate.

Smithsonian Science Education Center. **Weather Lab.** https://ssec.si.edu/weather-lab.

Additional Notes

The page references below provide answers to questions asked throughout the book. Questions whose answers will vary are not addressed.

Page 9: If the bowl were a lake, water would go up into the sky on a sunny day. Then it would come back down again. The model shows that water is always moving.

Page 11: Clouds might help you tell when it's going to rain.

Page 12: Airplanes that take long trips usually fly much higher than the clouds and weather below.

Page 13: Nimbostratus clouds would likely bring rain to the school fair.

Page 14: Ocean breezes feel cooler than the air on land.

Page 15: Inland areas generally get more rain and snow than coastal areas. **Page 15: Caption Question:** The pages would blow from left to right in the evening.

Page 19: Early settlers would have done best to settle where there was plenty of rain for crops—out of the rain shadow, on the west side of a mountain range. **Page 19: Caption Question:** The farm is likely on the west side of the mountains because that side gets more rain than the east side in the arid rain shadow.

Page 20: People in desert regions without large bodies of water would likely not go fishing, boating, skiing, or ice skating.

Page 21: It might be very hot, dry, and sunny in the desert, which could make going to an outdoor school fair feel very unpleasant.

Page 25: Evaporation happens even on a small scale.

Page 27: Condensation occurred on the plastic wrap. The plastic wrap represents clouds.

Page 28: A thermometer can help you tell whether it is warm or cool now, but not what it will be later, and it can't help you tell whether precipitation will fall.

Page 29: Melting ice caps might raise the water level in the oceans. Coastal areas might flood. People might have to move farther inland, and the weather patterns may change inland.

Page 33: A plane flying with the jet stream would go faster; a plane flying against the jet stream would go slower.

Page 34: Most weather patterns move from west to east.

Page 36: Rainy weather is likely. **Page 36: Caption Question:** On a warm spring day where the two fronts meet, there would likely be rain.

Page 37: Caption Question: It will probably be partly cloudy/partly sunny.

Page 39: High-pressure days are good for outdoor activities; low-pressure days are good for indoor activities. The school fair would go better on a high-pressure day.

Page 40: Knowing where the fronts are and how they are moving can help you predict when and where they will meet, and what the weather will be like when they do meet. Knowing where the low-pressure and high-pressure areas are can help you figure out whether an area might experience precipitation, also. **Page 40: Caption Question:** It would probably be snowing there.

Page 41: Satellite maps would use pictures to show the location of storms and clouds. By using maps from different times, you could tell in which direction the weather was moving, and how fast. Knowing all that could help you predict the weather on the day of the school fair.

Page 42: Doppler radar could help you see what weather is coming, and how quickly it is moving. You could figure out what weather will arrive on the day of the school fair.

Index